CW00328047

I ♥ SEX!

An Odd Squad book for RANDY RUMPY PUMPERS!
by Allan Plenderleith

ℛ
RAVETTE PUBLISHING

**THE ODD SQUAD and all related characters © 2005
Created by Allan Plenderleith**

First Published by
Ravette Publishing Limited 2005
Unit 3, Tristar Centre, Star Road, Partridge Green,
West Sussex RH13 8RA

Reprinted 2006

Printed and bound in Belgium

ISBN 10: 1-84161-241-3
ISBN 13: 978-1-84161-241-6

When the boss walked in, Maude was
backing up her stuff on a floppy.

Unfortunately, it was now pretty obvious
Jeff hadn't seen any action in a while.

To set the mood for love, Maude had
actually asked Jeff to put some BARRY White
on the stereo.

Jeff had no need for women, not now
he'd developed his very own set of 'beer boobs'.

Maude showed her love for Jeff by
giving him a big tight hug.

Maude had asked Jeff to give her
a quick bonk.

Sadly, Maude's impromptu booty shake had only succeeded in dislodging a surprise cling-on from within.

When Debbie got undressed, Dug discovered
she had a 'Brazilian' down there.

Maude's date looked different in the morning,
and had TERRIBLE breath.

Never blow off in the doggy position.

Having stopped for a quick wee, Jeff was
delighted when Maude gave him a special treat.

Jeff discovers where that spare condom had gone.

Jeff's boss could tell he had been looking
at internet porn again.

To find out if a man is going to be good
in bed, simply buy him a cream doughnut.

To her surprise, Maude arrived home to find
Jeff doing the dishes.

The JOY OF SEX
The REAL Positions!!

Spend Hours on Foreplay to Turn Her On

Satisfy Her Needs in Bed

Enjoy a Romantic Bath Together

Experiment with the 'Spoons' Position

Cover your Partner in Chocolate Sauce

Never Eat Curry the Night Before

Dug was pleasantly surprised when, during their love-making, Barbara started tickling his bum.

Using uncooked sausages and a filled bath, Jeff and Maude play the "Dunking-for-the-REAL-Love-Sausage" game.

Unfortunately, Jeff and Maude's first go with
a whip did not go as planned.

Dug discovers that if you go too deep during
oral sex the gag reflex can occur.

Jeff and Maude's romp in the back garden
had not gone entirely without incident.

During boring sex, Lily likes to pass the time
by playing with Alf's excessively hairy bum.

Maude was about to say how sexy the new jacuzzi was, when she noticed something.

To improve Maude's hand technique, Jeff
blocks up the end of the ketchup bottle.

On Saturday nights, Jeff likes to trick policemen
by boiling a kettle in his car and rocking it from
side to side.

If her date's shadow was anything to go by,
this was going to be one hell of a night!

Jeff finally finds a good use for his old,
unfashionably large mobile.

Jeff decides it's better to leave
the lights on during sex.

Alf spent all weekend deep inside Lily's bush.

The key to a loving relationship
is give and take.

How to have SEX when you're DRUNK!

I. BLURRED VISION IS A GOOD THING!

2. IF YOU'RE VERY DRUNK, YOU MAY BECOME SLIGHTLY CONFUSED!

3. KEEP ALL BOTTLES AND GLASSES AWAY FROM THE AREA OF ACTION!

4. BE CAREFUL OF OVER-ENTHUSIASTIC THRUSTING!

5. IF YOU'VE DRUNK TOO MUCH
IT MAY NOT BE A GOOD IDEA
TO JIGGLE ABOUT TOO MUCH!

Maude was with Jeff because in bed he
could perform magic with those fingers.

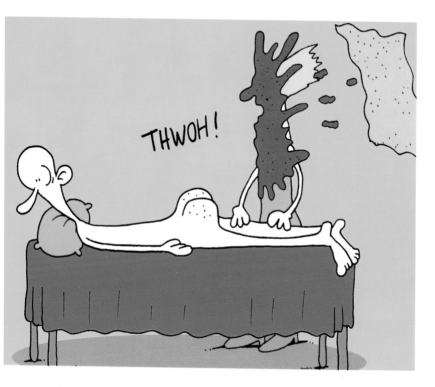

Unfortunately, during his sexy massage,
Jeff relaxed a little too much.

Although Maude thought she washed off all the chocolate body paint, she had missed a bit.

Dug discovers that sex dolls these
days are incredibly realistic.

To turn Jeff on, Maude dresses up in
her old school uniform.

Unfortunately, Jeff and Maude couldn't have
sex because she 'had the painters in'.

Why men should refrain from going for
a wee immediately after sex.

Suddenly, Maude's boss catches her
having phone sex.

Dug's attempt at the old 'hole in the
bottom of the popcorn box' trick backfires.

Maude surprises the postman on his birthday
with something warm and fluffy.

Suddenly, during her sexy dance, Maude's suspenders snap.

Jeff's dog learns the pitfalls of getting
jiggy with the sofa.

Although fun at the time, Maude later
regretted having sex on the stairs.

Unfortunately, Jeff's tan line gave away what they had been doing on the beach all day yesterday.

Maude awoke to find something tapping
her back, and it wasn't Jeff's hands.

Jeff couldn't understand why Maude refused to
have a look at his chocolate starfish.

SEXY GAMES!

THE 'SNEAK UPSTAIRS FOR A QUICKY WHILE THE RELATIVES ARE VISITING' GAME!

Maude learns why you should never
wear high heels in a waterbed.

The 'Who can do the Biggest Fart Game' goes awry when Maude loses control for a second.

Using an uncooked chipolata, Jeff fools Maude
with the old 'willy caught in the zip' gag.

Eek! Dug was sure Barbara had said she
was on the PILL.

Other ODD SQUAD books available ...

		ISBN	Price
The Odd Squad's Big Poo Handbook	(hardcover)	1 84161 168 9	£7.99
The Odd Squad's Sexy Sex Manual	(hardcover)	1 84161 220 0	£7.99
The Odd Squad Butt Naked		1 84161 190 5	£3.99
The Odd Squad Gross Out!		1 84161 219 7	£3.99
The Odd Squad's Saggy Bits		1 84161 218 9	£3.99
The REAL Kama Sutra		1 84161 103 4	£3.99
The Odd Squad Volume One		1 85304 936 0	£3.99
I Love Beer!	(hardcover)	1 84161 238 3	£4.99
I Love Dad!	(hardcover)	1 84161 252 9	£4.99
I Love Mum!	(hardcover)	1 84161 249 9	£4.99
I Love Poo!	(hardcover)	1 84161 240 5	£4.99
I Love Wine!	(hardcover)	1 84161 239 1	£4.99
I Love Xmas! (Sept 2006)	(hardcover)	1 84161 262 6	£4.99
The Odd Squad's Little Book of Booze		1 84161 138 7	£2.50
The Odd Squad's Little Book of Men		1 84161 093 3	£2.50
The Odd Squad's Little Book of Oldies		1 84161 139 5	£2.50
The Odd Squad's Little Book of Poo		1 84161 096 8	£2.50
The Odd Squad's Little Book of Pumping		1 84161 140 9	£2.50
The Odd Squad's Little Book of Sex		1 84161 095 X	£2.50
The Odd Squad's Little Book of Women		1 84161 094 1	£2.50
The Odd Squad's Little Book of X-Rated Cartoons		1 84161 141 7	£2.50

- -

HOW TO ORDER: Please send a cheque/postal order in £ sterling, made payable to 'Ravette Publishing' for the cover price of the books and allow the following for post & packing ...

UK & BFPO	70p for the first book & 40p per book thereafter
Europe & Eire	£1.30 for the first book & 70p per book thereafter
Rest of the world	£2.20 for the first book & £1.10 per book thereafter

RAVETTE PUBLISHING
Unit 3, Tristar Centre, Star Road, Partridge Green, West Sussex RH13 8RA

Prices and availability are subject to change without prior notice.